Spider Max, My Hero

Written by Anita Tendick

Illustrated by Sophia Patch

Copyright 2017
By Anita S. Tendick

All rights reserved.

No Part of this publication, Spider Max, My Hero, may be reproduced in whole or in part, or stored in a retrieval system, or transmitted in any form or by any means, electronic, mechanical, photocopying, recording, or otherwise, without written permission of the author.

Printed in the United States of America
University of Arizona Libraries
Tucson, Arizona
ISBN   978-1-940985-52-7
ISBN (E Book) 978-1-940985-60-2
Library of Congress Control Number: 2018967299

Acknowledgement

As I mentioned in the Acknowledgment of "Goodbye, Spidee Idee", I am not a lover of spiders. I do tolerate the smallest of the small, those I can barely see without my glasses. Anything larger creates varying degrees of stress, depending on the size! Amazingly, though, I have been inspired by my little arachnid friends to write my stories, despite my phobia.

In "Spider Max, My Hero", Max is a brave, anti-bullying soldier, who champions confronting a bully to encourage dialogue, trying to create peaceful co-existence. As a result of Max's efforts, Carly's little friend, Lizzie Lizard, and bully, Pete the Rat, become tolerant of each other and avoid further conflict.

So, to the spider species I am grateful. I hope you enjoy my stories as much as I have enjoyed writing them!

Come visit my website at www.anitatendick.com

Other books by Anita Tendick, illustrated by Sophia Patch are:

Goodbye, Spidee Idee

This book is dedicated to my wonderful daughter, Berkeley, and my two incredible grandchildren, Alex and Carly.

Spider Max, My Hero

By Anita Tendick
Illustrated by Sophia Patch

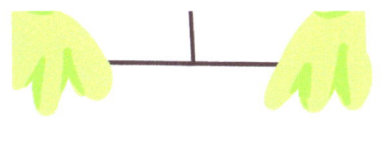

I called to my Mom when I came in the door, and I heard a loud noise, almost a roar! I followed the sound to the bathroom tub, and looked down to the bottom from up above.

And what did I see? I think you can guess! A little black spider, but not in a dress!! "Spidee Idee's cousin," I said in my head, "and it must be a guy, cuz he's wearing a tie!" And, WOW, what a tie!! With blues like the sky, reds like the sun when the day is done, and purples and greens like I've never seen!

He rose up on his back legs, as if to attack. Then flexed his muscles, and yelled, "I'm Spider Max"! The back of his red cape said "SM" in blue. Now I knew what it meant, and, BOY, was it true!!

I said in a soft voice, to help calm him down, "It's so nice to meet you. When did you get to town?"

"I came here from a city down in the drain. The very same city from where Spidee Idee came. The name of my city is Arachnoville, and many famous spiders live there still."

He relaxed a bit and he seemed pretty tame. So I asked if he wanted to know my name. "I think I can guess it," he said with great style. And I thought to myself, "We might be here a while."

He said, "It must be Emma", and I shook my head "no". "Then maybe it's Marjorie, Gretchen, or Jo?"

"Nope," I said. "But that's a good try".

"I thought I would guess it," he said with a sigh.

He was getting quite sleepy, as quick as that. His eyelids were heavy; he wanted to nap. So I said, "We'll talk later. I'll be back". I walked away quietly, as to not make a sound. I was so very happy to have Max around!!

I needed a new friend. I missed Spidee Idee. And Max was just perfect, so little and mighty!

I went out to play, then watched some TV. I went back to the tub, and he was looking at me. He said, " I know what your name is. I had just forgot. It's Iris, of course, like the flower in that pot!"

He was wrong, don't you know, but it was okay. I just wanted to be friends, and for him to stay. "It's really Carly", I said with a smile, "and I hope we are friends for a very long while."

He was happy with that and went back to his nap. I decided to wait, so I just sat and sat. He woke up again, more refreshed than before, and asked me to kindly show him the door.

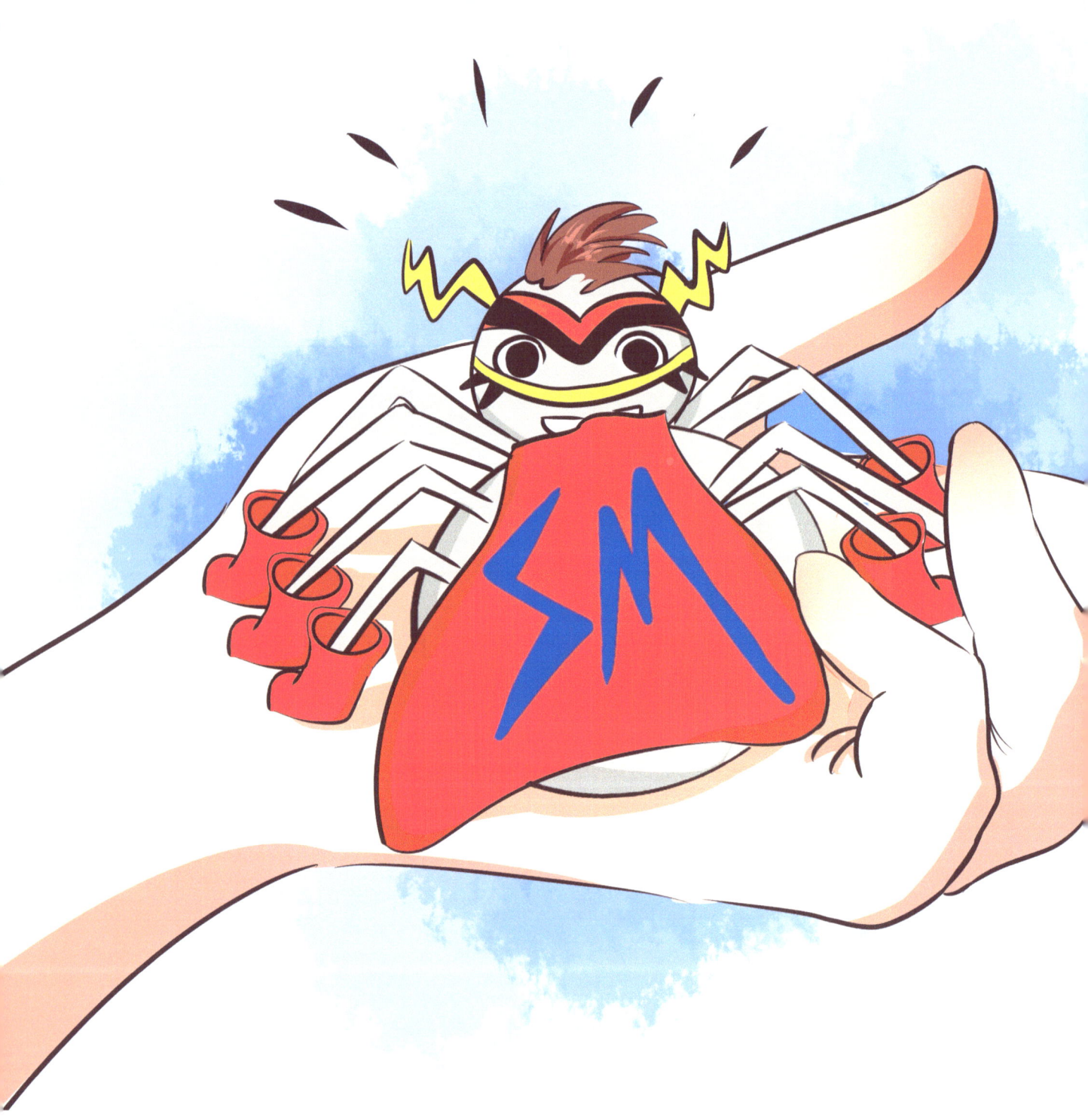

"Where are you going? Do you think you'll be safe? You are so tiny, and outside's a big place".

"Oh yes!" he said, "I fill others with dread, when I put on my mask and rotate my head!"

"Do you need a snack before you go?" He said he was full, but of what, I don't know. I asked what he ate down there in the drain.

He said, "It's a secret; it's hard to explain. You would think it is gross, cuz it's not like French toast."

"Ok", I said, "I don't have to know, as long as you're strong and continue to grow."

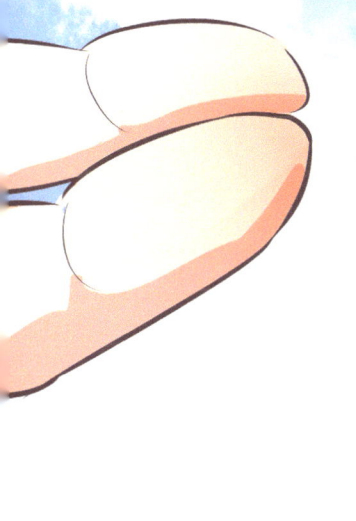

"Outside, Spider Max, I have a friend who hides. Not because she's shy, but this bully comes by, and says mean things to her, and makes her cry".

"I'm tough", said Spider Max, "and I'll help her be strong, because bullies are bad, and just do things wrong."

So he marched outside in his boots and his mask, and went looking for the guy who made Lizzie Lizard cry. "Where are you, big bully, who makes people sad? Show me your face if you're so tough and so bad!!

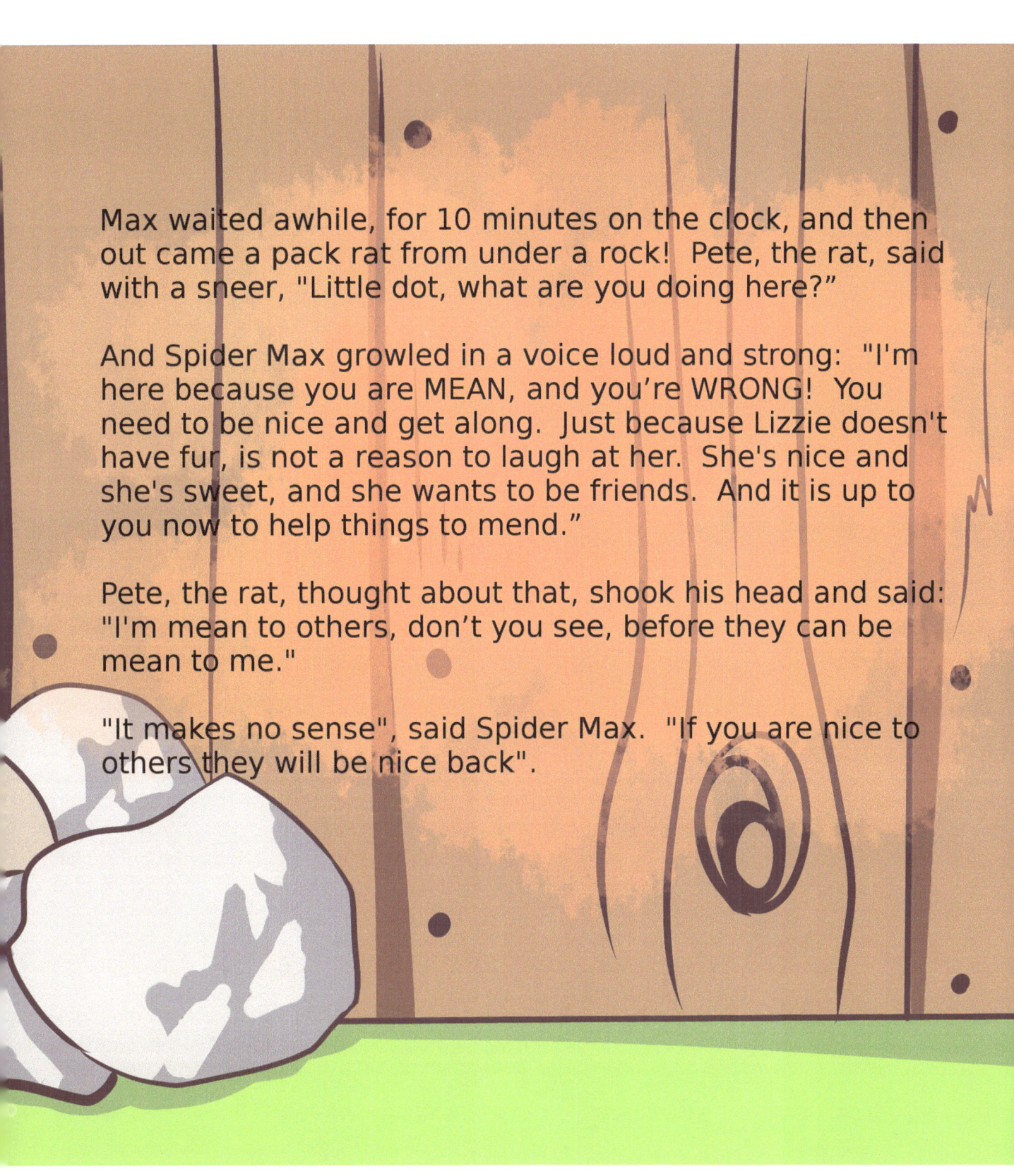

Max waited awhile, for 10 minutes on the clock, and then out came a pack rat from under a rock! Pete, the rat, said with a sneer, "Little dot, what are you doing here?"

And Spider Max growled in a voice loud and strong: "I'm here because you are MEAN, and you're WRONG! You need to be nice and get along. Just because Lizzie doesn't have fur, is not a reason to laugh at her. She's nice and she's sweet, and she wants to be friends. And it is up to you now to help things to mend."

Pete, the rat, thought about that, shook his head and said: "I'm mean to others, don't you see, before they can be mean to me."

"It makes no sense", said Spider Max. "If you are nice to others they will be nice back".

So Pete, the rat, though he didn't say, tried being nice the very next day. He smiled at Lizzie in a friendly way. Then they started to get along and even sang a friendly song: "Don't be mean, or push or hit, it puts you in an awful snit. Say good things, instead of bad, be nice to others and don't be mad. Then you'll have more friends, and we'll all be glad!"

They weren't BEST friends, I have to say, but they smiled at each other and went on their way.

Spider Max was happy, I could tell by his face. But he had to go on to another place. He packed up his suitcase, and winked his eye. I couldn't help it, I started to cry.

"Why, Spider Max, do you have to leave?" He smiled at me, and crawled up on my sleeve.

"Carly, you're sweet, and I hate to go. But I have to teach friendship to others, you know? The more friends we have, the happier we'll be. And maybe then, there won't be wars overseas. People will help others to plant food and be free; to make clothes and build houses, don't you see? And the one who can do this, is none other than ME!!"

So his work here was done, Pete and Lizzie were friends. "Goodbye, Carly, I'll come back again." And off he marched, my new hero and friend.

I'll always remember that little guy. Tough on the outside, but sweet as pie!!

Spider Facts

1. So what's so great about spiders? First, they eat insects – and lots of them. One spider can eat over 2,000 insects a year! Without them, your home and garden would have LOTS of flies, mosquitoes and beetles.

2. There are a few main differences between spiders and insects, and one of the biggest differences is the number of legs they have – all spiders have eight legs, and insects have only six legs.

3. Spider silk is extremely strong, and has a number of different uses.

4. One of the ways spiders use silk is to create webs, and these webs catch insects which provide food for spiders.

5. The silk strands in a web are five times stronger than a piece of steel the same size.

6. It takes a spider about an hour to build a web, and they usually build a new one every day.

7. Spiders lay eggs, and store them in an egg sac to keep them safe
.
8. Spiders have short hairs on their feet that allow them to walk upside down on ceilings and over glass.

9. The largest spiders are tarantulas, and the largest tarantula is the Goliath tarantula.

10. The average life of a spider is one or two years. But the female tarantula can live up to 20 years!

11. Tarantulas are really big and can be hairy. The biggest ones can eat a mouse or even a lizard. But they don't usually bother people, except they can look really scary!

12. In some kinds of spiders, the boy spiders are often much smaller than the girl spiders.

13. Most spiders have 4 sets of eyes. But they can be found in different places on the spider's head.

14. Even though spiders have eight eyes, most of them can't see very well – they rely on what they feel in order to know when they've caught food in their webs.

15. And the craziest thing of all: The blood of a spider is light blue in color! Isn't that weird??!!!

www.ingramcontent.com/pod-product-compliance
Lightning Source LLC
Chambersburg PA
CBHW050750110526
44591CB00002B/32